Mammoth Mammals

PATHFINDER EDITION

By Beth Geiger

CONTENTS

Mammoth Mammals

Long ago, Earth shivered through an Ice Age. And huge animals walked the planet.

~~~~~~~~~~~~ By Beth Geiger ~~~~~~~~~~~~

Imagine walking outside your house and seeing a 400-pound beaver with six-inch-long teeth. Or spotting a giant sloth eating treetops. Or watching a herd of woolly mammoths walking by.

Sounds unbelievable, doesn't it? But those animals were real. They lived from two million to ten thousand years ago.

The Big Chill

Those animals lived when Earth was much colder. That time is called the Ice Age.

What caused that big chill is a mystery. Scientists have lots of ideas. Many say Earth's **orbit,** or path around the sun, changed. As a result, less sunlight reached our world.

The change in orbit was small. But it made a big difference in Earth's **climate.** That's the pattern of weather over a long time.

Temperatures dropped. Snow and ice piled up, forming **glaciers.** Those huge ice sheets covered much of the Northern Hemisphere. Plants could not grow on the ice. Very few animals lived there either.

Areas close to the glaciers were also too cold for most living things. Farther away, however, some places were a little warmer. These areas teemed with life.

Cool Cat

Lots of animals lived in warmer areas far from the glaciers. Many were giant **mammals.** One of the fiercest animals was the sabertooth. Its fangs hung seven inches below its jaws.

This kitty weighed nearly 700 pounds. A sabertooth was too big to chase prey. Instead, the cool cat waited for dinner to come to it.

When the fierce cat spotted prey close by, it pounced. The sabertooth then used its long, pointed fangs like daggers. Those fangs slashed right through its prey. They could even tear open a woolly mammoth's belly.

On the Prowl. *Sabertooths pounce on a ground sloth. These were two of many creatures living on grasslands in South America.*

Where Were the Glaciers?

This map shows habitats during the Ice Age.

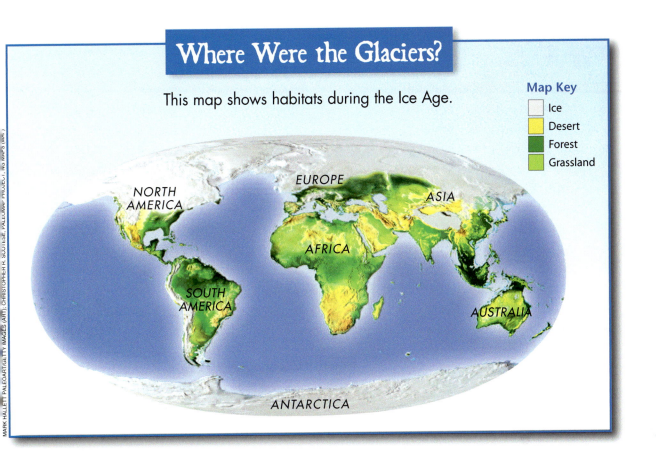

Map Key

- Ice
- Desert
- Forest
- Grassland

NORTH AMERICA

EUROPE

ASIA

AFRICA

SOUTH AMERICA

AUSTRALIA

ANTARCTICA

Woolly and Warm

One of the largest Ice Age animals was the woolly mammoth. It lived on cold, treeless plains called **tundra.** Mammoths looked like their modern relatives—the elephants.

Woolly mammoths were well suited for life in the cold. Their hair was three feet long. It even covered their toes. Under the hair was a blanket of warm, fuzzy wool. And beneath the skin was a thick layer of fat. The hair, wool, and fat kept the king-size animals warm.

The giant animals had long curved tusks. Each was more than ten feet long. The tusks were perfect for sweeping snow out of the way.

You might think those huge tusks would also be great for stabbing prey. But mammoths did not eat meat. Instead, they feasted on grass and other tundra plants.

Mammoths first lived in Africa. From there, they spread to other continents. They roamed Europe, Asia, and North America.

Ice Age People

Animals were not the only things walking the globe during the Ice Age. People lived alongside the supersize beasts.

These early people used spears to hunt the larger animals. They ate mammoth steaks.

People wrapped themselves in animal skins to keep warm. And they built houses from mammoth bones and tusks.

Pictures and Fossils

Ice Age people painted lifelike pictures on cave walls. These beautiful cave paintings show how some animals looked. Some of the pictures show giant bison and mammoths.

We can also learn about Ice Age animals from fossils. They are the remains of dead plants and animals. Fossils from Ice Age animals are found worldwide.

Some of the most famous fossils come from the La Brea tar pits. They are in Los Angeles, California. Long ago, Ice Age animals fell into the tar pits and died. The tar in the pits preserved the animals' bones.

Other fossils have been found frozen in the ground. In 1977, a bulldozer operator in Siberia dug up a frozen baby mammoth. It's the best one ever found.

The Heat Is On

Everything was going great for the animals of the Ice Age. Then about 10,000 years ago, something happened. Earth warmed up. Many of the creatures died out, or became extinct.

Chilled to the Bone.
Ice Age people use mammoth tusks to build a house. The tusks hold up a cover of animal skins.

What happened? Nobody knows. Perhaps the animals' favorite foods disappeared when the climate changed. Or maybe people overhunted animals. Then again, perhaps animals were just done in by disease.

One thing was certain. The Ice Age was over. The giant animals were gone. Warm winds melted the ice and blew plant seeds onto land that was once frozen. Soon new animals moved in to those places. Life went on. But it would never be the same again.

 Which Ice Age animal do you like the best? What makes it cool to you?

Wordwise

climate: weather pattern over a long period of time

glacier: giant sheet of ice

mammal: warm–blooded animal that feeds milk to its young

orbit: path around an object in space

tundra: cold, treeless plain

Meet the Animals

Sabertooths and mammoths were just two of many weird animals that lived during the Ice Age. Many were giants. Others just looked odd. Here are a few of those cool creatures.

Glyptodont looked like a giant armadillo. It was ten feet long and almost five feet tall. Armored plates covered the glyptodont's body. It even had a shield on its forehead.

Giant sloth was about the size of a modern elephant. It probably ate grass and low tree branches.

Titanis was a flightless bird. It had a nasty beak and an appetite for fresh meat. Almost ten feet tall, it could run 40 miles an hour.

Compare the Ice Age animals below with their modern relatives.

- Which pairs are related?
- How are the animals alike?
- How are they different?

Tiger

Tigers are the largest members of the cat family. Some tigers weigh more than 500 pounds. They have powerful jaw muscles and sharp fangs. Their long, strong legs allow them to run at high speeds to chase their prey. Tigers are one of the most endangered animals in the world today. The only remaining wild tigers are found in Asia.

Woolly mammoth Page 6

Giant sloth Page 7

Sabertooth Page 4

Today and Long Ago

Elephant

Elephants come in two kinds, African and Asian. These big-eared, long-tusked mammals are the largest land animals alive today. An adult male elephant can weigh more than 13,000 pounds! Elephants walk as many as 35 miles a day in search of water or food. They eat mainly leaves, twigs, and fruit. Elephants can live to be 60 years old.

Sloth

This shy, slow-moving mammal lives in the trees of Central and South America. Sloths grow to be about three feet long. That's about as big as a medium-size dog. Sloths spend their entire lives high above the ground. Sloths eat, sleep, and travel in trees. Their long, curved claws let them hang upside down from branches.

Where Did

During the Ice Age, North America was home to many strange and wonderful animals. Now most of these animals are extinct. What happened to them? Scientists think that many Ice Age animals died out quickly. They have several ideas, or theories, about why this happened.

Changing Times

One theory is that Earth's climate changed. It went from cold and icy to warm and dry. Scientists think these changes happened quickly. To survive, Ice Age animals needed to adjust to the warmer weather. But some animals may not have been able to adapt fast enough. Instead, they died out.

Other scientists think people are to blame. Humans began living in North America around the same time the animals started to die out. Maybe human hunters killed the animals off.

Surviving the Ice Age

These are just two theories. Scientists don't know exactly what happened or why. But one thing is clear. Not all Ice Age animals died out. Some were able to survive the changes that happened on Earth.

Today, some of their relatives still live in Africa. These survivors give clues about life in the Ice Age. They help us figure out why some animals might have died out. They also show how some were able to adapt and survive.

They Go?

Ice Age Survivors. *Today, rhinoceroses live in the warm grasslands of Africa. Their ancestors survived the Ice Age.*

Ice Age

What cool facts did you learn about the Ice Age?

1 What was the Ice Age?

2 When did the Ice Age end? What might have caused it to end?

3 How do scientists learn about the Ice Age?

4 What animals living today are similar to Ice Age animals? How do these animals compare?

5 What do scientists think happened to Ice Age animals in America?

© APHOTODISC